Moments of Color and Cloud

Moments of Color and Cloud

poems by
Gloria Heffernan

SHANTI ARTS PUBLISHING

BRUNSWICK, MAINE

Moments of Color and Cloud

Published by Shanti Arts LLC

193 Hillside Road
Brunswick, Maine 04011

shantiarts.com

Designed by Shanti Arts Designs

Cover image— Wendy Harris, *Winter's Last Blush,*
Used with permission of the artist; background and title
page— george-c-Yza / Q9v09KD0 / unsplash.com

Printed in the United States of America

ISBN: 978-1-962082-98-3 (softcover)

Library of Congress Control Number: 2026937362

Contents

Acknowledgments 11

Introduction: Exploring the Colors
    and Clouds of Aging 13

Aging Gracefully 15
Approaching 60 16
Thirty Minutes a Day 17
Wrong Turns 18
Family Tree 19
Twilight Garden 20
Mental Notes 21
Sieve 22
The Giveaway 23
Second Generation 24
Curb Appeal 26
Sometimes the Muse 28
This Too Is a Love Story 29
Melt 30
Wednesday Lunch Special 32
Enter Password 33
Visiting Sue at the Nursing Home 34
Deliverance 35
Love, Sue 36
The Visit 38
Autobiography in a Purse 40
Yellow Roses 42
Moments of Color and Cloud 44
Daffodils 45
Found Poetry 46
Flirtation 47
Saturday Morning Pilgrimage 48

Shopping for Sheets   49
Heiress   50
Heirloom   51
Lay-Z-Boy   52
Elegy for My Black Suede Pumps   53
Sorting the Clothes   54
Restoration   55
Kitchen Table Lament   56
Late January Again   57
Sally's Angels   58
Dawn Redwood   59
Before the Flip   60
Years Later   61
Invitation to the Estate Sale   62
I Believe in Old Hollywood   63
When I'm Sixty-Four   64
4,745 Cups of Coffee x 2   65
And He Loves Me   66
Pressing Issues   67
Last Poem and Testament   68
Love Letter to My Screaming Left Hip   70
Power Steering   71
Regrets   72
After the Beep   73
And Then My Feet Said . . .   74
Koan in the Bathroom Mirror   75
Diving In   76
In the Garden with Brayden   77
Insomnia in Real Time   78
Silence Interrupted   80
Barb at Seventy   81
Lenten Rose   82
Her Way   83
The Navajo Way   84

On the Avenue, 1938 — 86
Tuesday Morning at Debbie's Diner — 87
Packing It In — 88
Prom Night, 1977 — 89
Witness — 90
Crossing — 94
Polar Funeral — 95
Planning the Funeral — 96
Testament — 97
To You Who May One Day Be My Caregiver — 99

Acknowledgments

Animal Grace (chapbook; winner of the Keystone Chapbook Prize): "Polar Funeral"

Autumn Sky Journal: "Sieve"

Burningwood Literary Journal: "Kitchen Table Lament"

Certain Age: "Flirtation"

Fused (Shanti Arts Publishing): "Sometimes the Muse"

Gyroscope Review: "Autobiography in a Purse"

The Healing Muse: "Second Generation"

The Iris Literary Journal: "Lenten Rose"

Kosmos Quarterly: "The Navajo Way"

Moss Piglet: "In the Garden with Brayden"

One Art: "Heiress"; "Power Steering"; "Sorting the Clothes"; and "Years Later"

Quarter/ly: "I Believe in Old Hollywood"

Life Cycle Series (Pure Slush): "Planning the Funeral" and "When I'm Sixty-Four"

Still Crazy After All These Years: "Packing It In"

Still Point Arts Quarterly: "Moments of Color and Cloud" and "Yellow Roses"

Introduction

Exploring the Colors and Clouds of Aging

I didn't know I was starting to write a book when I wrote the poem "Moments of Color and Cloud." At the time, I was simply writing a poem to honor my friend Wendy Harris, an artist whose painting *Winter's Last Blush* graces the cover of this book. Wendy had been chronicling the many moods and hues of the sky for over thirty years. And then, at age seventy-five, she was diagnosed with Alzheimer's disease. I wrote the poem to offer her some words of encouragement and hope as she faced her diagnosis.

I didn't know that this poem would be a threshold into the complex landscape of aging. I hadn't begun to notice the colors and the clouds that were emerging throughout my writing. Poems about loved ones for whom aging was a continued ripening into wisdom and fulfillment. Poems about friends who were struggling with illness, isolation, and loss. Poems about the joys and anxieties of my own aging process. In recent years, I have had the privilege of witnessing the grace and vitality of my eighty-five-year-old sister-in-law Barbara, to whom this book is dedicated. I marvel daily at the ever-sharpening wit and creative energy of my eighty-two-year-old husband, Jim. I am invited to witness the dignity of friends who are suffering, and the loving support of those who care for them.

As these themes became more prominent, this book began to take shape. Not a book about the despair and decay of aging nor a fairy tale about the joy of our golden years. Age is too intricate a subject to reduce it to a simple category. And gold is too one-dimensional for this multi-dimensional time of life.

Aging encompasses a wide variety of elements—pain and joy, fear and hope, loss and gratitude. It is defined by a full spectrum of both colors and clouds. This book seeks to explore the process of growing older in all its richness, difficulty, messiness, and beauty.

Gloria Heffernan
Syracuse, New York
October 2025

Aging Gracefully

When I think of aging gracefully,
I visualize Katharine Hepburn,
shoulders erect, voice strong despite the tremor,
sweeping into a room on a wave of elegance.

I think of Audrey Hepburn who
never stopped carrying herself like a ballerina,
who never lost her radiant smile,
whether entering a ballroom or a mud hut.

I don't think of stray hairs sprouting from chins,
I don't think of cheeks descending into jowls,
I don't think of lips etched with spider webs
of lines that pinch into a perpetual pucker.

I wasn't particularly graceful at twenty and
glamour is a language I never learned to speak.
So I don't know why I expect to carry myself
like Kate or Audrey now in my sixties.

Perhaps I have been laboring all these years
under a simple but devastating typo.
Perhaps the goal, the prize, is to age
G r a t e f u l l y.

Grateful for each day, each breath,
Each beloved face I encounter,
Each tender word uttered or received.

Perhaps it is simple gratitude
that underscores all those other qualities.
Perhaps gratitude
is the very essence of grace.

Approaching 60 ❧

I wanted to stare sixty in the face and say,
What's in a number?
Having decided early that seventy years
would probably be enough for me,
I chose to have my midlife crisis at 35
when I had the luxury of
being told I was too young
for middle age.

But now, ten days before the end
of my sixth decade,
time grins knowingly from the top of the stairs
while I trudge up one step at a time
pausing periodically to catch my breath.

I want to resist its pull toward inertia,
but for now I do not revel
in the impending milestone.
Instead, I succumb to the weariness
of my fifty-nine years, eleven months,
and twenty days,
cheered only by the promise of a nap
when I reach the top.

Thirty Minutes a Day ∾

According to the *New York Times*
150 minutes of walking every week
will—not can—*will* stave off
heart disease, cancer, obesity,
depression and Alzheimer's disease.
I repeat these facts like a mantra
as I tie my shoelaces,
fill my water bottle,
reach for my keys.
150 divided by 7 equals 21.43
minutes per day.
I wrap myself in this simple equation
the way a marathon runner
wraps herself in a Mylar blanket
as I map out a route with just enough
incline to make it a challenge,
just enough flatland to make it inviting.

For decades the specter of exercise
has felt like punishment
rife with flashbacks
of Miss Higgins in her business suit
and polished white sneakers
brandishing a whistle and shouting
Faster, faster, as she threatened
ten more laps for anyone
who couldn't keep up.
21.43 minutes a day is not punishment.
Miss Higgins is long dead,
buried no doubt with her starter's whistle
threaded between her fingers like a rosary.
May she rest in peace
while I stride into the morning air
ready to save my life.

Wrong Turns

Lost in the city I have called home
for twenty years. I make one wrong turn
and then another and another until main roads
and side streets intersect into a series of dead ends.
I find myself in an abandoned parking lot.
Dueling highway ramps issue instructions
that read like remnants from The Tower of Babel.

The city has become foreign to me—
worse than foreign, because if I were lost
in Rome or London or Paris,
I could simply call it an adventure
and look for a charming cafe on a cozy street.
But here, so close to home, it is a haunting.

Multiple voices mock my efforts to find my way.
The GPS spews directions that sound increasingly
like my high school English teacher, Sr. Elizabeth,
telling me for the hundredth time that my sentences
have too many twists and turns for the reader to follow.
"Just get us from point A to point B," she would declare.
Perhaps she should have taught me Driver's Ed instead.

And then there's my own voice reminding me
about the article that said the first sign of dementia
is losing your sense of direction. I could take solace
in the fact that I have never had a sense of direction,
but instead I sink deeper into the maze of confusion
and the terror of being lost forever.

Family Tree

The Smoke Tree you planted
with your Dad five years ago
looks like a gathering of angels
all decked out in burgundy haloes.

Eight feet high and just as wide,
could you have imagined such grandeur
when you gave him the plastic bucket
that held a small bush with a Father's Day card
tucked into the soil?

I watched the two of you
sweating under the hot sun,
measuring the depth and width of the hole,
contemplating how unlikely it seemed
that this little shrub would ever require
so much room to grow.

Did its size surprise you
when you pulled into the driveway
for this year's Father's Day visit?
Now a father yourself,
you've come to appreciate
the miracle of growth.

Next time, you'll bring your boy
and show him where you and his grandfather
shoveled the earth onto a tarp,
watered the soil to ready it for new life,
covered the base with mulch to protect the roots.

You'll tell him about that hot day in June,
when grandpa taught you how
to plant a tree, and the joy
you shared in watching it grow,
the same way he has watched you grow,
the same way you watch your son.

Twilight Garden ∾

The Memory Care Center
looks out over an acre of wildflowers
populated with thousands of poppies
that spring up overnight.
A field we drive past every day,
suddenly awash in crimson.

They sway in unison
in the orange and purple twilight,
wave upon wave
of undulating red petals
interspersed with wild indigo
and forget-me-nots.

A bank of windows overlooks the meadow
that so easily could have been paved over
in favor of more parking spaces.
Instead, they chose to seed it with wildflowers
where hummingbirds and honeybees
can feed and thrive,
and residents can gaze out
over a tapestry of color—

a gift of now for those
who cannot remember when.

Mental Notes ≈

The mental notes I once relied on,
are now scribbled in disappearing ink
on discarded scraps of memory
left near an open window
on a windy day.

Sieve

Did I remember to lock the door?
Where did I put my glasses?
What was I looking for?

I was always a bit scatter-brained.
A missed appointment. A forgotten name.
Did I remember to lock the door?

You have a brain like a sieve, my mother said,
when I couldn't find the glasses perched on my head.
But what was I looking for?

Now with a Medicare card in my purse,
forgetfulness feels much more like a curse.
Did I remember to lock the door?

I wonder and worry, is this how it starts?
Losing keys and glasses and all my spare parts.
What was I looking for?

I know I came in here to find something.
Retrace my steps; start remembering.
Did I remember to lock the door?
Oh what the hell am I looking for?

The Giveaway

Some people call it downsizing.
She simply calls it the next step
as she lightens the load she will carry
to the assisted living community
down the road from her home of thirty years.

She extends an invitation to loved ones
to come and choose items
from the living gallery she has curated
throughout her eighty-three years.

She gives me a quilt she made by hand.
To her daughter, the collection
of blown glass paperweights collected
with Charlie during their three-decade marriage.
To her brother, all the tools and gardening supplies
used for a lifetime of spring plantings,
and their mom's mixing bowl that he cherishes
even though he never bakes.

Every gift comes wrapped in a story,
and as they are carried out to various cars,
she smiles and nods approval,
each item a liberation.

Second Generation

It was the second call that told the story.
Not the first one, when Bette told me
the diagnosis without naming the disease.
My oldest friend, mentor, Sunday school teacher.
The one who taught me to bake bread
and made the best corned beef and cabbage
this side of the Atlantic.
Today's call erased all doubt as she told
the same story she told me yesterday. Verbatim.
Oh well, she said. *It is what it is.*
And what it was. And what it will be.

> I was fifteen when she hired my mother
> to be a companion to her own mother.
> *Just keep her company,*
> *And make her a cup of tea in the afternoon.*
> *We don't like her going near the stove.*
> There wasn't a name for it then.
> But when my mother came home,
> she would tell me some story Bette's mother
> had told her—again—and how the words
> and inflection never varied.
> And how my mother listened,
> without finishing her sentences or reminding
> her that she already knew the story.
> She just laughed at the funny parts,
> and sighed at the sad, crocheting a blanket
> or folding laundry while she waited
> for the kettle to whistle.

The doctor says there are lots of new meds,
she tells me. *He says I'll be fine.*
Says he can tell I'm a real fighter.
And he's right about that.

She'll fight to keep her home.
Her car. Her cat. Her hope.
It's just a matter of attitude, she says,
convincing herself, if not me. So I listen,
just as my mother did fifty years ago.
I laugh at the funny parts.
Sigh at the sad.
Wait for the kettle to whistle.

Curb Appeal

I

Wheeling a wagon to the curb,
she waves us over with a friendly greeting
Welcome to the neighborhood, she declares brightly.
I'm Kit, and I'm ninety-one years old.
A fine network of crinkling lines emanates from
from the corners of alert blue eyes,
red lipstick, perfectly applied, maps a timeless smile.
She slides the trash bags from the wagon
and arranges them neatly at the curb.
Do you observe the cocktail hour?
I make a mean Manhattan, she chuckles,
Drop by any time.

II

She rolls her wagon to the curb.
A For Sale sign swings in the autumn breeze.
Oh yes, she chirps, *it's time,*
the lilting voice betrays not a hint of melancholy.
Alzheimer's you know.
She smiles to comfort us at the news.
My girls have made all the arrangements.
Memory Care, they call it.
She eases the trash bags off the wagon,
arranging them neatly by the curb.
Cocktails tonight? she chuckles over her shoulder.
We'll have to hurry before I forget!

III

A row of newly planted Black Eyed Susans
bloom in profusion along the driveway.
Grass mowed, doors locked, curtains drawn.
The daughters' cars are packed and gone.
No time for good-byes.
Soon their mother will not remember the new neighbors,
nor the punchlines of her favorite slightly bawdy jokes,
or the shafts of afternoon light
pouring through the picture windows
of the house she called home for sixty years.
By the curb, two trash bags
arranged neatly on a wagon.

Sometimes the Muse ⮢

is an 87-year-old man with Alzheimer's
who clutches the greased rope of memory
long enough to call and say,
Remember that thing you said about God?
And trust?
That was good.
Write a poem about that.

A poet himself, he doesn't remember
that he once wrote about the sequence
of flowers blooming seventeen miles a day
as Spring travels from South to North.

But he remembers that you asked him
if he still prays. He remembers that
you asked him to channel his trust in God
into trusting the loved ones
who remind him daily that who he was
remains who he is,
even if he forgets their names.

A preacher long ago,
he remembers congregations
who trusted him and how he earned that trust,
and how he loved their reliance upon him,
even as he resists relying on others now.

Remember that thing you said
about sadness, and about my wife
crying about the disease,
and not because I have let her down?
That was good.
Write a poem about that.

This Too Is a Love Story

She lifts the spoon to the lips
she has kissed for forty years,
wipes the soup from his white beard,
steadies him as he rises from the chair.

Ours too is a love story, she says,
especially now, so many years
after they said I do, lived each vow,
and now reside permanently
in sickness, not in health.

Ours too is a love story,
she reminds him
as she rereads his favorite poem,
retells stories of their shared past,
retrieves him from hallucinations.

Ours too is a love story, she says,
of the love that endures
even in moments when her face
is the face of a stranger.

Ours too is a love story, she says,
as she sits at the kitchen table,
sips tea that has grown cold in the cup,
listens for his voice down the hall,
studies the nursing home brochure.

Melt ⃛

Some memories have already
begun the inevitable melt
like glaciers calving into the sea.
What was the name of the iceberg
the size of Delaware that we photographed
from the cruise ship window?
How many countries signed
the Antarctic Treaty and when does it expire?
Already, I have forgotten
the markings that distinguish
the gentoo penguin from the Adelie,
the longitude and latitude
of frozen ports of call,
how many days Shackleton's men
were marooned on Elephant Island.

I remember cold.
I remember my hands cramping
inside clumsy insulated gloves.
I remember chapped lips that peeled
and bled from the wind,
the long slow sigh
of a humpback whale surfacing for air,
the clatter of penguins gabbling
in throngs on the beach,
the roar of two cantankerous
fur seals crashing their chests together
like cymbals.

I remember wonder.
I remember awe.
I remember the thunder of ice walls
crashing into the blue waters of Paradise Bay.

I remember days when the temperature
was warmer than my hometown
half a world away and how the snow
in my backyard doesn't just melt.
It recedes—gradually at first
until suddenly, without fanfare,
it's gone.

Wednesday Lunch Special ⁓

On Wednesdays, I visit Sue
at the nursing home with Rosie in toe.
As we walk past the dining room,
the manager squats and calls
Come here Sweetie,
so I drop the leash
and Rosie leaps into her arms.

The manager embraces the wriggling dog
and heads straight for the center table
where a silent woman contemplates her meatloaf
until Rosie rises up on her hind legs and gingerly
places her front paws on the woman's thigh.
She meticulously licks each finger,
an expression of love for both the elderly lady
and the gravy that still lingers on her fingers.

Laughter spreads around the table
as a smile spreads across her face.
Each diner awaits the chance to pet
the dog who obliges like an actor
willingly handing out autographs
at the stage door.

The manager clearly knows better,
even as she encourages me to stroll
from table to table in clear violation
of health department rules
about animals in the dining room.

She knows the ropes, knows the risks,
knows that she is on her own as she decides
what will really nourish those in her care.
The residents laugh and point and wait to be anointed.
Mashed potatoes later, the manager decides.
For now, the only item on the menu is joy.

Enter Password ⤳

Open Sesame doesn't work anymore.
Nothing is that simple.
Now it has to include a special character,
upper case letter buried in the middle,
exclamation point after every third letter
to confuse the hackers
who are far more likely than I
to gain access to my information.

Where did I put the question mark this time?
Did I use my birthday or my anniversary?
My dog died three years ago but his name,
followed by the pound sign
and the first three digits of my phone number
still grants access to my credit card statement.

Like the keys I have spent my whole life
losing and finding and losing again,
these enigmatic encryptions
keep me locked out of my own door,
and by the time I find the list where
I diligently record each and every one,
it's time for a security update
and!a???whoLe//new(*)start.

Visiting Sue at the Nursing Home ∽

She looks up when I enter, eyes bright when she sees me.
We exchange greetings and I avoid questions like,
What's new? or *How are you doing?*
sparing her the need to sigh and say. *Same old, same old.*

So I talk instead.

I talk to fill the silence,
To fill it like a suitcase I'm packing for a month-long trip.
To fill it like a house crammed with too much furniture,
To fill it like a shopping cart stuffed with junk food.

I talk because I forget the beauty of silence,
Forget to sit quietly at the edge of the bed and hold her hand,
Forget to absorb the silence like summer leaves absorbing sunlight.
Forget to let the silence hold us while the world goes noisily by.

Deliverance ⤳

As I walk the long hallway to her room,
I hear the carts delivering meals,
the nurses delivering meds,
the televisions delivering news.

I find her sitting in the wheelchair that has replaced the car
she once used to deliver groceries to a homebound neighbor,
To deliver her grandson to Little League practice,
To deliver herself to the church where she prayed for seventy years.

I sit beside her in the stuffy room
Delivering a small bouquet of supermarket carnations,
Delivering a hand to hold while we watch a Hallmark movie,
Delivering the only thing she wants from me—
a loving presence that says you are not alone.

Love, Sue ⤳

It is a small kindness—
A stack of Christmas cards, a list of addresses,
A conversation about who will receive them.

An hour sitting in the lounge of the nursing home
while carols play and nurses push wheelchairs
down narrow hallways.

She matches cards to recipients.
I write the salutations and pass her the pen
so she can sign

> *Love,*
> *Sue*

in the perfect Palmer penmanship
she reserved for birthday wishes and get well
cards and always-timely Thank You notes.

As the choreography of the pen
flows easily from hand to hand,
she pauses, looks at me, and says,

I want to send a card to you,
But I can't write all the words
I want to say.

So I let her words shower over me
the way her beautifully inscribed
notes once filled all those mailboxes.

I squeeze her hand, *You're welcome,*
I say, knowing that I am the one
who has received the gift.

She is not a portrait of decline.
She is a landscape in transition
picking up a new brush,
capturing a new moment,
and another, and another.

She is an alchemist who has spent her life
transforming paint into gold.
Now she faces a new canvas on which
she will transform loss into discovery.

The Visit

I am always prepared for it,
but this is the first time
I walk into the lounge
and see no light of recognition
in her eyes.
I wonder what she sees
when she twists her neck
and looks up at me through
eyes that have grown
cloudy with confusion,
narrowed with pain.

Ready for lunch? I ask brightly,
feeling her hesitation
in that brief moment
before she nods a cautious yes,
so tentative, but eager
to please the smiling
visitor who offers an arm
as she struggles out of her seat.

We walk slowly to her room.
I steady her with my arm
and adjust my pace to match
the halting shuffle that has replaced
her former gait, quick and sure
like the horses she used to coax
over hurdles and high jumps.

When we reach her room to gather
jacket and purse, I ask her the question
I dread. *Do you know who I am?*
She smiles the smile she has learned
to rely on when the answers don't come.

I tell her my name and watch the clouds part.
Of course! Of course it's you!
She still remembers how to hug
and throws her arms around me
as if I had just arrived with a bouquet
of spring flowers in the dead of winter.
Are you ready for lunch? I ask again.
Always, she says, rising stiffly.
Always.

Autobiography in a Purse

The first, a cast-off from my mother,
was filled with all the essentials
a five-year old needs to get through the day—
crayons, a Barbie doll, an empty lipstick tube,
also cast off, but still bearing traces of
Cover Girl Pink Carnation.

By high school,
it was a canvas bag
with shoulder straps
and patchwork pockets on the front
stuffed with pencils, notebooks,
mirror, and a lipstick of my own.

With my first job, I graduated to leather,
brown and supple with brass buckles
and ample room for a full-fledged make-up kit,
checkbook with my name printed on it,
and a matching—albeit empty—wallet.

Each year a different bag,
a different inventory of detritus—
ticket stubs, chewing gum wrappers,
a vintage subway token
found under a tear in the lining.

At sixty, a lighter purse—
pared down to the essentials.
Make-up kit edged out
by an eye-glass case.
Hand lotion and Chapstick
to defend against the elements.
Notebook and pen
for those fleeting ideas
that seem ever more elusive.

Each decade,
the purse is a little smaller,
a little lighter,
more economical in its contents
as I choose more carefully
what's worth carrying
into seventy.

Yellow Roses

It peeks out from an assortment of
mismatched dishes on the fifty-cent table
like a time-traveler that journeyed from
a tenement in Jersey City
to a yard sale in Syracuse—
a voyage not of miles but decades,
and still in full bloom.

Two yellow roses curve on the edge of the plate—
identical to the ones my mother
piled high with mashed potatoes and meatloaf
in the kitchen on Duncan Avenue
more than sixty years ago.
No nicks or cracks to betray its age—
only a few scars from knives
dragged across the petals.

Uncovering the roses was the reward
for cleaning our plates,
and woe to the child who failed to finish
in our waste-not, want-not home.

For half a dollar, I ransom memories
more nourishing than all the meals
this plate has ever held.
I consider hanging it on the wall
over the kitchen table,
but reject the notion.

Instead, I slide a fried egg onto the plate
while my tea steeps on the counter
and I wait for the toast to pop up,
just as my mother did
on countless Saturday mornings
when she called us to the table
for breakfast in a garden of yellow roses
blooming on a vinyl tablecloth.

Moments of Color and Cloud ❧

She is closing her studio,
removing the paintings from the walls,
adjusting to the reality of Alzheimer's disease,
a moniker she wears now
the way she has worn Artist for forty years.

Her canvases shimmer with light and shadow,
the dew-drenched radiance
of an Adirondack lake at dawn,
a two-lane highway unfurling
between fields of new-mown hay,
a pillar of sun piercing the blue
and crimson clouds of twilight.

She is a curator of moments.
Moments of blessing, moments of pain.
moments that beg to be recalled,
and moments that, once lost,
will never be missed.

These are not paintings.
These are moments of color and cloud.
These are the ineffable
rendered into the timeless.

Lost keys, irretrievable passwords,
a pot left too long on the stove,
a face untethered from a name.
An inventory of evidence
verifies the diagnosis.
But a diagnosis is not an identity.

Daffodils

On the day we help her move out,
the daffodils she has tended for years
have opened alongside the front porch
like a row bright yellow teacups
brimming with sunshine.
I don't point them out fearing
they might produce a stab of regret.

The assisted living community,
which I refuse to call a facility,
is just a mile down the road,
but so far away from this sunny
ranch house she has lovingly tended
for three decades.

When we arrive in the parking lot,
I steal a nervous glimpse her way
and see her wearing a radiant smile.
Oh look, she proclaims with delight,
pointing at a fresh patch of daffodils
blooming beside the front porch.

Their bright yellow petals
wave in the breeze as if
heralding our arrival.
It looks like they just opened up
to welcome me home.

Found Poetry

Poetry found me in the 25-cent bin
at the Salvation Army Thrift Shop
on a summer day in 1967
when I unearthed a book
that smelled of dust and cigarettes,
with notes scribbled in the margins
and pages folded down at the corners.

In the five-hundred page
Treasury of British and American Verse,
I found Shakespeare and Robert Frost,
Walt Whitman and Edna St. Vincent Millay.
I discovered "The Quality of Mercy,"
trod "The Road Not Taken," heard
"The Song of Myself," and discovered
"The Courage that My Mother Had."

Too young to understand
most of what it held
I kept turning the pages,
reading the words I could read,
puzzling over what was new
and incomprehensible
until I found
"The Midnight Ride of Paul Revere,"
with its irresistible invitation:

Listen my children,
And you shall hear . . .
And I did.
And I still do.

Flirtation ❧

Mrs. Riley was right.
In sixth-grade Home-Ec class,
she looked at my loopy lop-sided stitches
and with her hands on her hips,
shook her head in disgust and said,
Don't you even know how to flirt?

Well, no. I didn't.
And apparently,
I didn't know
how to hem a dish towel either.

A hem must be subtle and ladylike, she said,
pursing her maraschino lips.
*It must be strong enough to keep things in place,
but dainty enough to be invisible.*

Fifty years later,
I have jettisoned dish towels
in favor of the dryer cycle
on my dishwasher.
I take my skirts and slacks
to the tailor when they need
to be hemmed.

I still don't know how to flirt
but I have learned
in my own loopy and lop-sided way
that I never needed that particular skill.
And being invisible was never
all it was cracked up to be.

Saturday Morning Pilgrimage ⧽

Twice a year, when I visit my great-nephews,
Saturday morning is reserved for breakfast at the diner.
We rise early and make the half-mile pilgrimage
while they debate who will sit next to me,
and then discuss what they will order
knowing they are free to get anything on the menu--
even as I chafe under the sure knowledge
that most of the potatoes will be left behind
in a pool of ketchup,
and the fresh squeezed orange juice
will likely spill during a game of Hangman
scrawled on the back of the paper placemat.

When the food comes, we don't say grace
although I season my scrambled eggs
with a healthy sprinkle of gratitude
as I watch the boys anointing their pancakes
and French Toast with floods of syrup.
This ritual has no liturgy. We don't
kneel and rise at prescribed intervals.
And when we hear bells, they simply announce
order up and not the arrival of the Holy Spirit.

But the feast we share at this communion table
is a sacrament nonetheless—a sacred act of praise,
with every bite a hallelujah.
Munching my whole wheat toast, I know
that someday they will bring their children,
just as I brought their mother,
to a diner in some small town or big city
where they will recall breakfast with Aunt Gloria
who will hover in the aroma of coffee and bacon
like the fragrance that lingers in the church
long after the incense has ceased burning.
And to that I say, *Amen.*

Shopping for Sheets ∾

100% Wrinkle Resistant!
boasts the package of microfiber bed linens.
You pay extra for this feature
which offers a smooth surface,
but leaves your back sweaty
with microplastics that don't breathe.

But bedtime is no time for resistance.
So I move down the aisle to the cotton sheets
that will no doubt ball up in the dryer
and fit my bed like a topographical map
of hills and valleys.
Wrinkled, but fresh and natural.
Cool in the summer,
Warm in the winter.
Growing softer with time.

I take my purchase home
and wash them before tucking them in
under the lumpy mattress.
As night falls, I feel no resistance
as I slide between the layers
of cool cotton fabric,
and rest in my wrinkles.

Heiress

For twenty years, my sister's fine china
has sat dormant in my kitchen cabinet
until this morning when a steady rain
tapped at the window and I sipped my
Earl Grey tea from one of the delicate cups
with its matching saucer.
Was it the rain that moved me
to take the cup from its shelf and
admire the lavender and mauve flowers
curling around the gilt-edged rim?
Or was it the thirst for memory?

When she died, each place setting
was still carefully packed away,
swaddled in pink tissue paper
and stored in the original boxes.
On the underside in gold lettering
the long-forgotten name of the pattern
sparks a rueful smile: Heiress.
I sip the tea and think of all
I have inherited from my sister—
so much more than a cup or plate
will ever hold.

Heirloom ∾

The quilt Beth made for me
is casually folded
over the arm of the couch
as if it weren't a work of art
but simply a blanket
meant to warm me
while I read a book
or sip my tea.

Over a year in the making,
it graced the worktable
in the sewing room
where her machine
overlooks the garden
that inspired the floral squares
she stitched together
into a cascade of burgundy rosettes
and pink geraniums.

It will outlive me
like the quilts of pioneer women
stitched over a century ago
hanging on museum walls
as if made only to be seen.

This heirloom
is meant for greater things
like warming Daniel
while he naps on a snowy day,
unaware that someday
it will belong to him,
and better still his grandchildren
whom I will never know.

Lay-Z-Boy

It was quite simply the ugliest chair in the world.
Dark green rocker recliner
with all the refinement of a hay bale.
Oversized, overstuffed, over-tired,
wisps of batting poking through seams
like tufts of hair protruding
from an old man's ear.

Ugly.
No other word for it.
Too big for the room where it took up
most of the floor space,
always gouging the wall
whenever I pushed it back to recline,
squeaking like a mouse with a megaphone
as it rocked back and forth.

When I came home
from the hospital that day,
I slumped into its lumpy cushion
and wept into its soft shoulder
while it rocked me to sleep.
That big beautiful ugly chair,
taking me into its embrace
as if my comfort was the only thing
in the world that mattered.

Elegy for My Black Suede Pumps ❧

Cradled in their cardboard casket,
they rest in peaceful repose
on the highest shelf of my closet.
No more the elegant elongation of calf.
No more the graceful arch of a ballerina *en pointe*.
These shoes that promised to caress my sole,
crushed my toes in cruel contortions.

With a wistful sigh, I close the lid,
and donning a pair of practical Birkenstocks,
or sneakers, or worse yet . . . loafers,
I visualize the sensibly shod
fairy godmother wistfully shaking her head
as Cinderella's glass slipper shatters on the palace steps.

The magic was never in the shoes, she sighs,
as the would-be princess picks the shards
from her shapely toes.

Sorting the Clothes

When the time came
to clean out your apartment,
I was efficient.
Because efficiency was what was called for.
Because efficiency was what I could handle.

I filled the giant trash bags by category.
Some would be hand-me-downs—
Some donations—
Some, just the things you never got around to throwing out.

Simple enough, until I held each item
and remembered the time you wore this dress to the theater,
or when you bought that tee-shirt on vacation in Quebec
or when you purchased the too-big sweater on clearance because
There's no such thing as too much cashmere!

Clothes that still carried your DNA,
Or the forgotten scent of a perfume you used to wear,
Or the faint ghost of a stain left behind after a wonderful meal.

I bundled up all the cozy sweaters and flannel nightgowns
and the fluffy bathrobe you wore all winter,
and labeled them for the women's shelter
just the way you told me to when you said,
We girls have got to stick together.

And when the bags became too heavy to lift,
I turned off the light and prepared to leave.
But first, I slipped the cashmere sweater
on top of the bag marked Shelter.

Restoration

I don't remember when it broke or how—
the statue of the Infant of Prague my mother
gave me more than forty years ago.
But I remember gathering up the pieces,
frantically reaching under the bed and nightstand
heedless of the sharp edges,
slipping the shards into a white cotton sock
to keep them from getting separated,
swaddling it between two thick sweaters
in the bottom drawer to prevent further fracture.

I kept it in that drawer for decades,
until the day I watched you repair
the porcelain frame that held our wedding picture
with such tender care and measured pace,
your patience as you held each fragment
in place until the bond was permanent.
When I asked you to restore my mother's gift,
you withdrew the fragments like an archaeologist
unearthing an ancient treasure with nothing
but tweezers and glue and steady hands.

Now I keep it on a high shelf safe from traffic
where no one can see the delicate web of cracks,
or the hole in the back where the tiny bits
had shattered into such fine powder
they couldn't be repaired, but you gathered them
like gold dust and poured them into the cavity,
restored, repaired, remembered.

Kitchen Table Lament

I miss the black wrought iron fire escape with its steps
that rattled outside the kitchen window on its way
up to the tenement roof top.

I miss the twin bed next to the kitchen table where
my mother slept and tried to convince me (and herself)
that it was just like the sleeping alcove in an old Irish cottage.

I miss the washing machine next to the sink
that she camouflaged with a pretty table runner
and a vase of plastic daisies whenever it wasn't in use.

I miss the contact paper behind the stove that she changed
every now and then to convert the cracked plaster walls into
brickwork or wood grain depending on her mood and what was on sale.

I miss it all except the roaches. Not even through nostalgia's
gauziest lens could I ever miss them. Even now, fifty years later,
I would still tell those roaches to go straight to hell.

Late January Again ❧

Late January points to Spring the way a compass needle points North.
The snow on the fairway has begun to recede.
This morning, wind blew clouds of white powder
across the hillside like sand across a dune.
The days grow longer despite the cold.
Just last week, five o'clock brought the weight of darkness
and today, that same hour is washed with pink clouds.

Late January used to mean birthday brunches at Tavern on the Green.
Icicles that fringed Central Park like diamond earrings in the sun.
I would spend weeks shopping for the perfect gift.
Now the date on the calendar cuts like a knife.
No longer a time to celebrate your life.
The day comes and goes like the wind and snow.
I lift a single glass of wine and raise a toast to memory.

Sally's Angels

When the contents of Sally's house
on Victoria Place were put up for sale,
I braved the long line of shoppers.
Some were just curious
about the treasures the old house held.
Some were looking for a good deal
on antiques or works of art.
I was there to buy one of Sally's angels.

Sally wrote poems about angels,
and her home was a testament
to her unfailing faith in them.
She believed they surrounded her,
and I believe she was right.

The one I chose is a musical snow globe
that plays "Hark the Herald Angels Sing."
She holds a banner bearing the word Joy
spelled out in gold capital letters.

It's the only Christmas ornament
I keep out all year.
It helps me see angels.
And hear them.
And remember Sally.

Dawn Redwood

Like a covert operation,
I drive past our old house slowly,
hoping that as I turn the corner
I will still see the Dawn Redwood
we planted on our wedding day,
when we poured my mother's ashes
into the bowl of earth
inviting her to nourish its roots
and bless our marriage.
Little more than a shrub when we planted it,
the top branches reached above the roof
the day we posted the For Sale sign.

We watched it grow from spindly spine
to solid trunk with branches
bending in a breezy ballet
over the impatiens we planted
at its base every summer.
Each time I turn the corner
I hold my breath for just a moment
remembering the exuberant new owner
who chattered joyfully about
felling the tree to make room
for a jungle gym and another
family's memories.

Before the Flip ⤬

No, you don't have to take off your shoes
before you begin your walk-through,
but I do wish you would find
a gentler way to walk all over me.

Before you declare my kitchen a total gut-job,
take a look at the oven, quite serviceable
despite its absence of stainless steel,
and still able to turn out a bubbling lasagna.

And when you visualize the new farm sink
with touch-free faucet on your list of must-haves,
notice that this one still runs clean clear water
to fill a kettle for tea with a friend.

Of course, the Formica countertops *must* be replaced
with top-of-the-line maintenance-free quartz.
Just look at the stains from all those messy ingredients
that went into decades of Sunday suppers.

Next, the master suite—oh, but there isn't one,
just a bedroom where a husband and wife
nestled against each other in the night,
untroubled by the absence of a walk-in closet
or *en suite* bathroom with jetted soaker tub.

There's no media room, or separate office, or home gym,
and I'll admit, my front yard is a tad lacking
in curb appeal. But don't demo me just yet.
A family spent a lifetime in this ever so humble home
where Open Concept applied only
to their hearts and minds and hands.

Years Later ⤳

In another room,
at the other end of the house,
my husband talks on the phone
for an hour with his ex-wife
discussing the joys and sorrows,
wonders and worries of their children,
the oldest of whom is fifty-five.

A frequent enough occurrence,
I have grown so accustomed
to their conversations
that I sometimes forget to marvel
at the way they navigate
the geography of family,
even as I joke that their divorce
is far more harmonious
than many marriages I have seen.

Even now, thirty years after they ceased
being husband and wife,
they have never stopped being curators
of what they co-created,
parents, separate but together,
like the coiled strands of DNA
that course through
the generations.

Invitation to the Estate Sale

Don't be shy.
Come in and browse for a while.
No need to be embarrassed.
I always loved a good clearance sale.

If those throw pillows will look perfect
on the couch in your den
where you have your morning coffee,
by all means, buy them.
You can never have too many throw pillows—
despite what my husband may tell you.

And don't feel funny about trying out
the recliner in the guestroom.
After all, you are a guest.
And it was my favorite place
to sit and visit with an old friend
who came up for the weekend.

As you pass through the kitchen,
choose a coffee cup or better yet, two—
it's always nice to have an extra for a friend,
and perhaps a couple of dessert plates to match.

Feel free to have a seat
on the sofa in the living room—
even if you don't think you'll buy it.
It's comfortable; that's why it's here.

So come on in. Don't be afraid.
You are not walking on my grave.
You are leafing through my scrapbook.
In the end, it's all just stuff anyway.
But such lovely stuff, isn't it?
And who doesn't love a good bargain?

I Believe in Old Hollywood ❧

I believe the book is always better than the movie
but the movie is still pretty damn good.

I believe Chitty-Chitty Bang-Bang would beat
James Bond's Aston Martin hands down.

I believe Rhett Butler really did give a damn
but there's only so much a man can take.

I believe in the collective gasp
when Dorothy's black and white world shifts to Technicolor.

I believe Lassie and Rin Tin Tin would have created
a magnificent litter of superhero puppies.

I believe in the soaring soundtracks and sweeping vistas of Westerns
but I always root for the Indians.

And I believe Lauren Bacall's husky voice oozed more sex
than all fifty shades of grey combined.

When I'm Sixty-Four

As my sixty-fourth birthday dawns,
I don't think this is what the Beatles had in mind-
me shivering under three layers of blankets
you asleep in the chair at the foot of the bed,
both of us coughing like seals stranded on a beach,
too tired for cards or cakes,
sharing the last of the cough drops and Kleenex.

You apologize for the absence of gifts, balloons,
all the usual accoutrements of celebration.
And I think of how many worse ways there are
to spend a birthday. Just as we have navigated
the lockdown, we navigate the virus.
Together. Taking turns making tea,
watching British detective shows,
doing crossword puzzles, being grateful.

What more did you think I might want?
How better could you have answered
Lennon and McCartney's question as you
spoon the tea bag out of the cup and
declare without words that yes,
you still love me when I'm sixty-four.

4,745 Cups of Coffee x 2 〰

Enough caffeine to keep us going
through all these thirteen years,
sweetened not by granules swirled in with a spoon
but the face above the rim,
the face that says good morning,
and reads the paper,
and does the crossword puzzle in ink,
and always takes time to laugh at the funnies
no matter what screams from the headlines,
the face that still warms and excites me like
a double cappuccino festooned
with cinnamon and extra foam.
This is the part where a lesser poet
might be inclined to say
My cup runneth over,
but not me.
I'll just say I love you,
pour in the milk,
and stir.

And He Loves Me ❧

He loves me.
Slender legs and slim hips,
Perky red pixie cut,
Lipstick, a tangy shade of strawberry.
I am the whole package
wrapped up with a pretty pink bow.
And he loves me.

Fifteen years later
Legs and hips are thicker,
Hair back to the original brown,
threaded with strands of silver,
Lipstick, an occasional afterthought.
Same package but the wrapping paper
is frayed. The bow, faded.
And he loves me.

So many changes over time,
But here he is, still by my side,
a mystery I need never solve,
a gift I re-open every day.

Pressing Issues

The pillowcase smooths out
like a snow-covered field
right before my eyes.

With a fluid motion, the iron glides
across the fabric, like a skater
practicing figure eights on fresh ice.

With the touch of a button
steam engulfs the toughest wrinkles,
leaving a flawless surface in its wake.

I, who opted for permanent press
decades ago, had forgotten the satisfaction
of a well-pressed crease.

Now I embrace what I once thought a chore,
grateful that in this world so full of troubles,
some small problems can still be ironed out.

Last Poem and Testament ∾

When you finally get around
to packing up the last vestiges
of scraps and mementos
I once thought important,
don't be surprised
when you find a scribbled note
tucked into the bottom
of my underwear drawer.
Just unfold it to see
what I left behind
in some forgotten
attempt at a poem.
And this is what it will say . . .

Thank you—
no more, no less.
Thank you for gusts of wind
spewing spindrift into our faces
on the shore at Pemaquid.
Thank you for Mountain Avens
and Ladies Bedstraw
springing up between the stones
of the Burren.
Thank you for climbing
776 steps of the Eiffel Tower
to watch dusk drape itself
over Paris like a shawl.
Thank you for midnight sun
in Iceland and micro-orchids
in Puerto Rico.

Thank you for home—
for handhewn birdhouses
and tulips every spring,
for snow tires on Valentine's Day –
a more practical way to say
I love you.
Thank you for every thing
that made this life
just a little harder to let go of,
and thank you most of all
for making heaven
feel downright
redundant.

Love Letter to My Screaming Left Hip ≈

You know what, Pain?
I really hate your guts.
But I realize now that without
your constant nagging,
I might not have gone to the doctor.

If you didn't keep waking me up
in the middle of the night,
I might have let this whole
osteoporosis thing get out of hand.

If you had let me keep ignoring you,
I might have wound up in a heap
at the foot of the stairs with a fracture
that could have been avoided.

Who knows? Maybe all your tormenting
was really just your way of saying,
Listen to me! Something's going on here.
It's time to take care of yourself.

Were you really just trying
to get my attention?
Was this just your way
of telling me you love me?

Power Steering ⤳

When I was six years old,
my mother bought a used
two-tone Chevy Impala
with power steering for $200.
Power steering.
She said the words as if they possessed
magical powers. She tingled as she
described in vivid detail the newfound
ease of parking and switching lanes
without the resistance of the ancient
Buick she had traded in.

As a child, I couldn't appreciate
the power of steering.
Even now, I tend to forget
that I have the power to steer
my thoughts from the dark
cratered roads where I too often
get lost or stall out. I forget
the sheer power of steering
when my brain wanders from one
overwhelming thought to the next,
and I find myself dwelling
on past wrong turns and flat tires.

Now when I turn the key in the ignition,
I try to remember that my mind
is not a driverless vehicle.
I have the power to steer my thoughts
in the direction of gratitude,
in the direction of hope,
in the direction of joy.

Regrets ⮀

If anyone should ever ask
what I most regret,
it will be the stories
I didn't tell.

The story of the dream I had
the night before Jackie died.
The way he stood
at the foot of the steps
bathed in white light—
even his sneakers gleaming.

I'm all right now, he said,
after the long months
of suffering and surgeries.
It's okay.

When his mother called
the next morning
to tell us he had died,
I never told her
that I already knew.

Never said,
Don't worry. He's okay now.
Never tried to explain
why I didn't cry
when I heard the news.

And now she too is gone.

After the Beep

Twelve years after his death.
it is still his voice
on the answering machine.

You've reached Don and Dottie.

Sometimes she calls the number
just to hear him say her name.

Leave a message after the beep.

Sometimes she does.

And Then My Feet Said . . .

No.
No to Barbie's arch arches
No to stilts and stilettos
No to teetering on tip-toe
No to bondage and bandage
No to straps that strangle
No to buckles that bite
No to looking stunning as long as I stand still
No to glass slippers that shatter on palace steps
No to corns and callouses, bunions and blisters
No to limping

Yes to leaping
Yes to toes fanned out in cool grass
Yes to running and jumping
and sweating and stinking and soaring
and dancing and strolling and jogging,
and splashing and stopping at nothing.
Yes to sneakers and slippers,
good sensible loafers with dependable
soles that embrace my soul.
Yes to getting there.
Yes.

Koan in the Bathroom Mirror

When I didn't like
what I saw in the mirror,
I stopped looking.
When I stopped looking,
I began to see.

Diving In

When was the last time
I opened myself to cool blue water?

Waikiki, San Juan,
the Greek Islands, Key West—

My tastefully discrete swimsuit
has traveled the world,

but never emerges
from my luggage.

The hot sun slicks my shoulder
with sweat while I swelter on dry land.

What secret do I think I am keeping
in that suitcase?

That my sixty-five-year-old thighs jiggle
and rub together when I walk?

That my rear is well-padded and rotund?
That my belly is more than ample?

The water doesn't care.
Why should anyone else?

In the Garden with Brayden ∾

Because no one has taught him yet
that women are supposed to look a certain way,

Because he has not read the magazines
that proclaim belly fat as the enemy of all things beautiful,

Because he hasn't learned that women should not have
a fine line of dark hair above their upper lip,

Because he doesn't know what the world
will be only too happy to teach him,

my five-year-old great-nephew
bends down in the garden

to admire the white hyacinth
at the edge of the daffodil bed,

and looks up at me declaring,
It's so pretty . . . just like you.

Insomnia in Real Time ✑

1:46 a.m.
My mind wanders, wonders.
Leaps from crisis to crisis.
Climate catastrophe.
Another election season.
There's a drought somewhere.
And wildfires. And space junk
falling from the sky.
And I don't dare turn on the TV
because some market research group
has clearly done a study that proves aging
insomniacs are more susceptible to images
of suffering and therefore more likely
to *Call the number on the screen right now.*
And then there are the infomercials
that look so promising at 2:00 a.m.
And a siren has just screeched past
heading to some tragic scene somewhere
and I'm lying here under my warm blanket
feeling sorry for myself because I can't sleep.
And now it's 2:30 in the morning
and I am no closer to drifting off
but I remember that scene in *White Christmas*
when Rosie Clooney and Bing Crosby
are eating liverwurst sandwiches
and drinking milk—real milk, not skimmed,
and they start singing about falling asleep
counting their blessings. And so, I do,
because Rosie and Bing wouldn't lie.
So I think of my beating heart.
My breath. My loved ones. My home.
I start wondering how high I can count
but I come back to this moment.
This blessing. Right here. Right now.

And I still can't sleep.
But oh God, how grateful I am.
And who can sleep with all these
blessings to tally up? And it's been years
since I had a good liverwurst sandwich.

Silence Interrupted

I remember the silence
        of a shallow pool among the rocks of Sabino Canyon.
        Sycamores, saguaros, and a stillness so deep
        it was shattered by the thrum
        of butterfly wings fluttering past my ear.

I remember the silence
        of a late-night subway platform,
        far below the midnight city streets
        just before the A-train roared into view
        obliterating the momentary quiet.

I remember the silence
        of early morning meditation
        before the ceaseless sound of tinnitus arrived
        like the flat-line tone of a heart monitor
        announcing the death of silence.

Barb at Seventy

The lighthouse beaming
intermittently behind her
is no match for the light
that beams within her –
constant, bright, tested and true,
penetrating the darkness
and overcoming countless storms.

Barb at seventy
revisits the rocky shores
that punctuate her memories,
scaling the promontory
that stretches out
at Pemaquid's feet,
where massive ribbons
of grey granite
shimmering slick
like a whale's back beckoning
break the surface
inviting her to climb aboard.

And so she does,
stepping gingerly at first,
and then taking command,
the purposeful stride
as ageless as these rocks
and just as strong.

Lenten Rose

for Pat Gregg, botanical illustrator

See her bent over the drafting table
examining unearthed specimens
of peony, orchid, dogwood
at the altar where she presides
over the perfect marriage
of art and science.

She celebrates the tangled roots
no less than the dramatic blooms,
each vein rendered with reverence
and precise accuracy
even where the Japanese beetle
chewed a peephole
into an irresistible leaf.

Hellebore, the Lenten Rose,
jewel of the winter garden,
slow to bloom,
resilient in the face of drought,
stronger than its delicate appearance
would suggest,

fitting model for an artist
whose hands bore the hell
of rheumatoid arthritis,
wringing beauty from agony,
fingers gnarled and twisted
like the tangled roots
that flourish in the dark.

Her Way

Whenever I hear the opening notes of "My Way,"
I hear the muffled catch of my mother's breath
as she covers her face with her hands
and says, *Don't look at me,*
I'm fine. It's just this damn song.

I hear my older sister ask,
Do you want me to change the channel?
as we watch *The Ed Sullivan Show*
like we do every Sunday night
waiting for Topo Gigio, or a band of acrobats.

I hear my mother snort
with something like a laugh as she says,
No, no, I'm fine,
and I believe her because I haven't learned yet
that *fine* is a code word for
There are some things I just can't talk about.

I hear the raspy voice of the glamorous singer
holding that long final note as my mother
wrings the wadded tissue in her hand,
exhales a long plume of smoke, and says,
especially when a woman sings it.

A million questions rattle my brain
as Ed goes to commercial
and my sister goes to the kitchen
to get a glass of water for my mother
who looks at me with a forced laugh and says,
Don't worry Sweetie.
Someday you'll understand.

The Navajo Way

Dark eyes averted,
tongues silent,
the children listen
as their grandmothers
taught them to

while the schoolteacher
prods and pushes,
demanding answers
to validate her
good intentions.

Listening to the Earth
they trust the answers
to reveal themselves
in the stories of the elders,
the bird song at dawn.

Listening to experts
she dictates answers
trusting in tests
to measure
the immeasurable.

In the schoolyard
the grandmother peers
into the classroom
remembering the
boarding schools,

remembering beatings
for speaking in her
mother tongue,
remembering teachers
demanding obedience,

remembering children,
dark eyes averted,
tongues silent,
awaiting the inevitable
emergence of truth.

On the Avenue, 1938 ⟿

The word dapper might have been invented
just for them,
strolling down 5th Avenue,
maybe to the Plaza for a Tom Collins
and then to the Village for some cool jazz.

Going forward, always forward,
she with her white hat and matching gloves,
he with a fedora on his head
and her on his arm.

The sweethearts, Doris and Milo,
who became Mr. and Mrs.
and then Mom and Dad,
and finally Greema and Da.

It's as if they can see it all stretched out
before them on that broad avenue,
smiling as they walk in unison
going forward, always forward.

Tuesday Morning at Debbie's Diner ❧

It's not about the coffee.
Frankly, I've had better,
but at least it's hot and plentiful
and the cups are always clean.

And it's not about the French Toast,
although it is delicious,
dripping with maple syrup,
and a crispy side of bacon.

It's all about the way Deb pours your first cup
without needing to ask what you want,
and how she knows you take Equal
and puts it on the table before you even ask.

It's about the way she knows that your second cup
will be decaf and she starts brewing a fresh pot
when she sees you're halfway through your first
so you won't have to wait.

It's about the way she banters with the table of ten
Vietnam Vets who meet here for breakfast
every Tuesday and how she calls them each by name
and refills cup after cup no matter how busy.

It's about every get-well card and every dollar
stuffed into the jar on the counter
when she was in the hospital with lung cancer,
and the way her regulars rallied round her
after all those years and all those breakfasts.

It's about the way her eyes say *I love you too*,
as she moves from table to table serving food
and smiles and the occasional wisecrack,
Because just like you,
she knows it was never about the coffee.

Packing It In

Chafing under the word retirement,
she packs up the accumulations
of a three-decade career

organizing papers
leaving lists of deadlines
and dead ends

re-reading a few thank you notes
filed away to remind her
that it mattered

she turns in her keys
and parking permit
feeling like a prehistoric creature—

the mighty thesaurus rex
seeking out new words to devour
not quite ready
for extinction

Prom Night, 1977 ∽

"Look . . . to go through life and call it yours—your life—
    you first have to get your own pain." —Peter Shaeffer, *Equus*

Early May in Jersey City.
My best friend and I are waiting
for the bus into Manhattan.

A stretch limo sails up to the stop light
and six of our classmates,
(I never did call them friends)

roll down the windows
waving and shouting
as if they are simply saying hello.

Catherine and I are dressed in our own finery—
no sequins or chiffon, of course,
but dressy enough for a night out on Broadway.

Waves of laughter bubble from the limo
long after the light changes.
They aren't bullies, really. Probably.

Maybe they really are just saying hello,
too caught up in their own excitement to notice
that we are heading to a different destination.

We could have opted for *Annie,*
or *Beatlemania,* or even (gasp) *Oh, Calcutta!*
But we aren't looking for song and dance numbers.

We spent the money we hadn't spent on prom gowns
to buy third row tickets for *Equus,* the gut-wrenching play
that might just prove there are worse things

than being eighteen years old and
not being asked to your senior prom.
Even today, I think it was money well spent.

Witness

I

My mother died
a year before the Towers fell.
I imagine how she would have
sat by the TV watching bodies
rain down from the sky.
How she would have rocked
back and forth on the edge of the bed,
her left leg shaking as her foot tapped out
an anxious Morse code on the floor
waiting to hear that I was safe,
her hands trembling,
inhaling cigarette smoke
exhaling prayers
until finally she would have muted the TV,
unable to endure the voices of the newscasters,
watching instead the silent images
until the pictures were seared into her brain.

II

At 9:15 the girl with long black hair
stands on the corner of West 4th and Mercer
watching smoke
pour out of the gash in the side
of the bleeding building.
My father works there, she stammers,
pounding the keypad of a mute cellphone
while it is still early enough for us
to believe it's a terrible accident.
He's not answering.

III

F-16s shriek over the silent city
audible because every other plane
on the continent is grounded and
the cars have screeched to a halt
on Sixth Avenue where Army jeeps
are the only moving vehicles
and a soldier young enough to be my son
directs the pedestrian traffic
in full battle gear.

IV

Ryan is walking near Bleecker Street
staring downtown at the now empty sky
no way to get to his dorm on Water Street.
Deaf, he cannot hear the F-16's flying overhead.
Lost on the familiar streets,
he is trapped in a horror movie
with the mute button pushed.
Second week of sophomore year
he knows the neighborhood
but can't find true south
on the city's compass.

I shepherd him to my apartment
where he hunkers into the corner of the couch.
I think of his mother whom I cannot call
because the phones are not working.
For the first time, she knows his deafness
from the inside out—
she cannot hear the only words that matter to her:
Your son is safe.

He holds Duncan on his lap
clutching the dog who
let's himself be kneaded,
burying his nose into the angle
of the boy's elbow.

V

Sheri has walked from 44th and Broadway
to my apartment on Greene Street
heading south into the smell of
burning jet fuel that has wafted the three miles
north to Greenwich Village
where it will linger for weeks in the air,
years in the memory.
She passes Washington Square Park—
suddenly a photo gallery of the missing
spontaneously erupting on the chain link fence
surrounding the Arch.
Candles and bouquets litter the sidewalk
where silent witnesses gather for solace.

VI

My mother died
a year before the Towers fell.
Every year, I picture her
as she would have been,
sitting on the side of the bed,
smoking, trembling, remembering
FDR's voice telling a grieving nation
of a day that would live in infamy.
I think of college students
who were children when the Towers fell,
whose mothers silenced the news reports until
after they had gone to bed,

sheltering them from the images
that would shape their future.

They know 9/11 the way I know Pearl Harbor—
Through the stories of those who witnessed it,
those who inhaled the smoke
and dust and cremated remains
of 3,000 mothers and fathers
and accountants and salesmen,
those who watched the muted news reports
until the pictures were seared into their brains,
those who woke up on a brilliant September morning
to find themselves suddenly in the crosshairs.

Crossing

I don't know what happens
on the other side of the threshold
between life and death.
Of course, I have heard the stories.

In those final moments, they say,
the dying will look up toward the ceiling
and smile—just the way you did.

I wondered who had arrived in your line of vision
in that room, so dark and quiet,
where the only sounds were your slow breaths
and the steady hum of the monitor
that measured your weakening heartbeat.

Was it your mother calling to you
as she did when you were taking your first steps?
Or some anonymous angel whose presence embodied
all the love you had ever known,
all the peace you had ever sought.

I don't know what you saw,
when you turned your head to the left
and gazed past me up to the ceiling.
But I know what I saw.

I saw peace. I saw relinquishment.
I saw permission to surrender your hand
to the grasp of whoever had arrived
to carry you over that threshold.

Polar Funeral

In the wind I hear stories
of Eskimo elders who,
sensing their time was near,
wrapped themselves in seal skin robes
and set out on an ice floe
to let the wind and water
carry them home.

I wonder if I might do the same—
If this flesh that has housed me
for so many years might have
one more chance to be of use.

I wonder if my body,
after I have no more need of it,
might be dropped from a helicopter
onto a northern ice floe
where a starving polar bear
might feast on my remains.

I wonder if I might be served up
as penance for a warming planet—
If I might offer my cold flesh
to preserve that majesty and grace.

Planning the Funeral ❧

Easier than planning a wedding.
No seating chart or RSVPs.
And yet, there are arrangements to make.
Guests to consider.
And of course, the dress.

She tells me the plans
over tea in her quiet den.
Would you like another cookie, dear?
After my polite reply,
she returns to the subject at hand.
Pink flowers, she declares.
All pink. Roses, lilies, the whole shebang.

And the 23rd Psalm, of course.
Not because it's customary—
just because it's the cornerstone
of her ongoing conversation with God.

She has chosen a favorite poem
to be read from the altar,
a poem she wrote herself for the occasion.
After all, she giggles. *I want to be there, too!*

I am puzzled by the ease
with which she navigates her agenda.
Should I change the subject?
Comfort her with assurances of longevity.
Remind her she is the picture of health
and has nothing to fear?

But she has no fear.
Needs no assurances.
At eighty-seven, she is ready for the journey,
and planning her farewell party.
I just like to leave things tidy, she says.

Testament

I have always wondered why they call it a will—
As in where there's a will there's a way
As in the spirit is willing but the flesh is weak
As in Thy will be done.
As in what will I do without you?

But despite the discomfort, we do the mature thing.
We have the necessary conversations.
We make our wishes known and afterwards,
we toast ourselves with a nice chardonnay.

But I am not ready for this will
nor for all it will not.

It will not fill the empty space beside me
when the time comes to read it in a tastefully furnished,
book-lined office where worldly goods will be allocated,
papers signed, condolences offered.

It will not make me laugh out loud
at inappropriate moments as you so love to do.
It will not hike an Adirondack trail in Autumn.
It will not gaze with wonder at the Northern Lights.

It will, of course, give me security and
it will stand as a testament to a love story
that will continue long after the end.

But that end will demand that I live on without you—
without the certainty that when I walk through the door
you will be there waiting to help me put away the groceries—

That when I wake in the morning,
you will sit across from me at the table
drinking your coffee and reading the funnies—

That together we will plant another season of annuals
alongside the perennials we have tended together,
that have grown such strong deep roots over the years.

To You Who May One Day Be My Caregiver ⤳

They say that life is not a dress rehearsal.
But what if it is? What if the lost keys,
the misplaced glasses, the name
that doesn't come readily to my lips
are just Act One in a play I never want to star in?
What if I am slowly learning the lines
I will one day perform for you,
an audience of one, watching from the front row
day after day for a very long run?

And so, I rehearse the thing that terrifies me
more than anything in this terrifying world.
I visit dear friends who live in the shadow of memory
as they perform their own long final act,
the ones who trust me to be
not only audience but companion,
not only companion but witness,
not only witness but student.

The ones who teach me to face each moment with grace.
The ones who dare me to find joy in a future
I would too readily dismiss as hopeless.
The ones who have begun their journey back in time,
whose memory of this morning's breakfast has fled,
but who can tell you the area code and number
of their very first telephone.
The ones who teach me patience
as I listen to them retell the same stories,
ask what day it is, introduce themselves
as though we have never met before.

If it ever happens to me, my dear,
I want you to hear this now
while I can still weave words into a blanket
that will keep us warm in the cold we might face together.

Know that I trust you to do what you must when the time comes.
Know that I trust you to keep me safe whatever it takes,
even when that means trusting others to do the job.
Know that I trust you to remember me as I am now,
and to remind me, again and again and again,
when I can't remember on my own.

Gloria Heffernan is the author of three previous poetry collections, most recently *Fused* (Shanti Arts Publishing). Her craft book, *Exploring Poetry of Presence* (Back Porch Productions) won the CNY Book Award for Nonfiction. She has received the Naugatuck River Review Narrative Poetry Prize, and numerous Pushcart Prize nominations. Gloria is the author of the collections *Peregrinatio: Poems for Antarctica* (Kelsay Books), and *What the Gratitude List Said to the Bucket List,* (New York Quarterly Books). Her work has appeared in over 100 literary journals and anthologies. She is co-editor of the forthcoming anthology *Now I Chant Old Age: Poems of Mindful Eldering,* with Phyllis Cole-Dai. Gloria also teaches poetry workshops, facilitates writing retreats, and provides editorial consulting services. She lives in Syracuse, New York, with her husband, Jim, a lifelong academic who is the designated first-reader for all of her poems. To learn more, visit: www.gloriaheffernan.wordpress.com.

Shanti Arts

Nature · Art · Spirit

Please visit us online
to browse our entire book catalog,
including poetry collections and
non-fiction books on nature, healing,
art, and more.

Also take a look at our highly
regarded art and literary journal,
Still Point Arts Quarterly, a feast for
the eyes and the imagination —
available to download for free.

www.shantiarts.com